KNOWSLEY LIBRARY SERVICE

Knowsl@y Council

Please return this book on or before the date shown below

weblinks

You don't need a computer to use this book. But, for readers who do have access to the Internet, the book provides links to recommended websites which offer additional information and resources on the subject.

You will find weblinks boxes like this on some pages of the book.

weblinks

For more information about village landmarks, go to www.waylinks.co.uk/ GeogDetective/Villages

waylinks.co.uk

To help you find the recommended websites easily and quickly, weblinks are provided on our own website, **waylinks.co.uk**. These take you straight to the relevant websites and save you typing in the Internet address yourself.

Internet safety

↗ Never give out personal details, which include: your name, address, school, telephone number, email address, password and mobile number.

↗ Do not respond to messages which make you feel uncomfortable – tell an adult.

↗ Do not arrange to meet in person someone you have met on the Internet.

↗ Never send your picture or anything else to an online friend without a parent's or teacher's permission.

↗ If you see anything that worries you, tell an adult.

A note to adults
Internet use by children should be supervised. We recommend that you install filtering software which blocks unsuitable material.

Website content

The weblinks for this book are checked and updated regularly. However, because of the nature of the Internet, the content of a website may change at any time, or a website may close down without notice. While the Publishers regret any inconvenience this may cause readers, they cannot be responsible for the content of any website other than their own.

WAYLAND

THE GEOGRAPHY DETECTIVE INVESTIGATES

Villages

Ruth Jenkins

WAYLAND

First published in 2007 by Wayland
Reprinted in 2008
Copyright © Wayland 2007

Editor: Hayley Fairhead
Designer: Simon Morse
Maps and artwork: Peter Bull
Cartoon artwork: Richard Hook

Wayland
338 Euston Road
London NW1 3BH

Wayland
Level 17/207 Kent Street
Sydney, NSW 2000

Jenkins, Ruth, 1978-
   Villages. - (The geography detective investigates)
   1. Villages - Juvenile literature
   I. Title
   307.7'62

ISBN 978-0-7502-5050-4

Printed in China

Wayland is a division of Hachette Children's Books,
an Hachette Livre UK company
www.hachettelivre.co.uk

Picture acknowledgements
Cover: St Nicholas church in the centre of the village of West
Tanfield, Wensleydale, Yorkshire.
For permission to reproduce photographs, the author and
publisher would like to thank: Ian Beames/Ecoscene: 21t.op; Frank
Blackburn/Ecoscene: 21b; Michael Boulton/Pictures of Britain: 17b
Steve Bryant/Pictures of Britain: 19t; Bryn Collton/
Assignments/Corbis: 13; Ashley Cooper/Corbis; front cover, 10;
Danita Delmont/Alamy: 28; Colin Garratt/Milepost 921/2/ Corbis:
17t; Jason Hawkes/Corbis: 9b; Jon Hicks/Corbis: 4; Gavriel Jecan/
Corbis: 29; Michael Jenner/Robert Harding PL: 25; Martin
Jones/Corbis: 9t; Tom Kidd/Alamy: 12; John Lawrence/
Stone/GettyImages: 1, 8; Niall Macleod/Corbis: 11; Manor
Photography/Alamy: 22, 26, 27; Sally Morgan/Ecoscene/Corbis: 20;
Tony Page/Ecoscene: 14; Richard Passmore/GettyImages: 18; Dave
Pattison/Alamy: 23; Photofusion/Alamy: 15; Picturepoint/Topham: 24;
Simmon Aerofilms Ltd/Alamy: 6; Spectrum/HIP/Topfoto: 5; Patrick
Ward/Corbis: 7, 19b; David Woodfall/Stone/GettyImages: 16.

Contents

Words that appear in **bold** can be found in the glossary on page 30.

Answers to Sherlock Bones' questions can be found on page 31.

What is a village?

A village is a place where people live or a **settlement** that has at least 100 inhabitants. Settlements with fewer inhabitants are called hamlets, settlements with more inhabitants are towns. There is usually a church, public house and other local **services** like a post office, garage or primary school in a village.

FOCUS ON

Different settlements

A hamlet is smaller than a village – with no shops or services. A town has a larger **population** and more shops and facilities. A city normally has over 100,000 inhabitants, a large range of shops and often its own cathedral or university.

The settlement of Bamburgh village, Northumberland is centred around Bamburgh castle.

The place where a village is built is known as a **site**. Village sites can be found anywhere: near to the sea or inland, on mountains or in valleys. There are several factors that influence people when they choose their site. The first relates to defence. Farmers used to live together in groups so that they could defend themselves and their property more easily during times of war.

People look for sites that are dry and free from the threat of **flooding**. This means that people sometimes build on small hills so that their homes do not flood.

Despite the risk of occasional flooding, some villages are built near rivers as they are a good source of water, which is needed for many things from generating power to providing drinking water. If you study a map of an area with chalk and **limestone** hills such as the Mendips or North Downs, you will see lines of villages along the base of the hills. This is because springs emerge from underground at the base of these hills. The spring water is rich in minerals, and is often bottled to be sold in shops. This helps some villages to make money.

Other factors that determine site location include: a good supply of wood for building and fuel; and rich, fertile soil that is good for growing crops or grazing animals.

Formerly a small village, Leamington Spa in Warwickshire developed into a large town after spring water was discovered there.

How are villages laid out?

Villages are usually laid out in a pattern influenced by the shape of the physical features around it – such as a river or hill. You can normally see this pattern if you look at a map or aerial photograph of the area. However, as a village grows and more buildings are constructed, this pattern may become less obvious.

DETECTIVE WORK

Investigate the patterns of villages near to where you live. Find a map of your local area at your library. Look at the patterns on the map. You could also look at maps on the Ordnance Survey website. To find out more, go to:

weblinks

www.waylinks.co.uk/series/
GeogDetective/Villages

An aerial view of South Zeal village in Devon. Houses follow the line of the main road through the village.

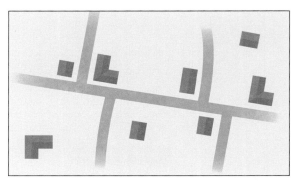

A dispersed village

A nucleated village

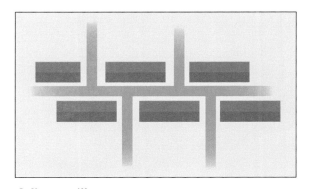

A linear village

There are three main types of **settlement** pattern: **dispersed**, **nucleated** and **linear** settlements.

Dispersed villages are spread out with no real pattern as the houses are spaced far apart. They are thought to have developed where woodland was cleared for animals to graze.

Nucleated villages have buildings that cluster around a central point, perhaps a road junction or **village green**. Nucleated villages were safe during times of trouble as people could work together to guard the village people and houses. A nucleated pattern helps villages to develop a sense of community. Homes may be built around a building that is central to the community such as a church or village hall, so people are more likely to meet each other when they are moving around the village.

Linear (or ribbon) villages grow in a long line along a river, road or valley. This is often because the land either side of a river or along a valley floor is the flattest land available, and this is much easier to build on than land that is sloping.

Can you work out the settlement patterns for the villages shown on pages 6 and 7?

Houses in Saint Buryan, Cornwall spread outwards from a church at its centre.

What types of houses are there?

The different houses that you find in villages give clues about how villages have grown and when the most growth took place. As the **population** of a village increases, new houses have to be built to accommodate the extra people.

Traditional thatched cottages are often associated with villages. **Thatching** is a type of roof covering made from dried plant material like straw, water reeds and heather. It is a very old type of roofing that is becoming popular again because it is attractive and environmentally friendly. Thatch helps to keep houses warm in winter and cool in summer and the materials are also available naturally. Today, there are more thatched roofs in England than in any other European country.

Two thatched cottages in Welford-on-Avon, Warwickshire with well tended gardens.

FOCUS ON

Holiday homes

Attractive village houses are sometimes available for rent during holiday periods. This enables people who don't live in villages to experience village life first hand. Renting out village houses is an important source of money for some people in **rural** areas.

These almshouses in Surrey, date back to the seventeenth century.

Some villages have **almshouses**. These are small houses, sometimes within a **terrace**, that are designed to provide a home for those who are poor. They are normally run by charities. In the UK, they date back to the tenth century and help people to remain part of their local community even if they can't afford to pay full rent.

New houses are built as more people move into a village. These houses can be built in **cul-de-sacs** on the edge of villages or in terraces in the centre. In certain areas, villagers worry that modern houses make the area less attractive. However, new homes are sometimes built to look like the older, more traditional houses in the village.

DETECTIVE WORK
To find out more about villagers' concerns over houses being built in a Welsh village, go to:

weblinks

www.waylinks.co.uk/series/
GeogDetective/Villages

This housing estate has been built at the edge of a village.

What landmarks can you find in villages?

The church in West Tanfield, Yorkshire.

Village landmarks play a central part in the identity of many villages. Landmarks can be either natural features or man-made buildings or monuments.

Landmarks built by people give an important insight into the history of a village. A village's most prominent building is normally its church or chapel. Church towers and steeples are visible from far away, and the sound of church bells can be heard for miles around. They are a focal point for many families: churches are where people worship and celebrate, are baptised, married and buried. Sunday morning services are an important occasion for many villagers. Each church is unique, and is usually home to detailed records of many generations of villagers.

DETECTIVE WORK

Can you find the story behind a famous landmark in a village near to where you live? Look out for clues on buildings, such as dates on walls or plaques that describe part of the building's history.

The Half Moon pub in a Buckinghamshire village. Pub signs are interesting landmarks to look out for.

Other important landmarks to look out for in villages include: war memorials to those villagers killed in the two World Wars, houses of famous people, pubs and village halls.

Village halls are an essential part of village life. They are used by the community as a venue for clubs such as youth clubs, evening classes and drama productions. **Village greens** are also a focal point in many communities. A common sight on Saturday afternoons in summer is cricket being played on village greens.

What are village schools like?

Most villages have a local primary school, but few have enough residents to support a secondary school. This means that children have to travel to a larger village or town to go to school when they have finished Year 6. To help make this journey easier, some local councils provide buses or taxis to get village children to school.

FOCUS ON

Attendance at school

The oldest village school in England is Ewelme School in Oxfordshire, which began in 1437. However, as many children were needed to work on the farms at that time, particularly during the harvest, attendance was sometimes poor. It was not until the early twentieth century that all children had to go to primary and secondary school.

Children wait for the school bus on the Isle of Jura, Scotland.

Some schools have a very small number of pupils, and are costly to run. This makes it difficult for them to survive. There are currently 2,700 schools in England with less than 100 pupils. Today, children in villages travel an average of 5.1 miles to get to school, almost double the distance children have to travel in cities.

DETECTIVE WORK

Find out where your classmates travel from and how far they travel:

1. Enlarge a map of the area around your school using a photocopier – up to A3 size if possible.
2. Highlight the location of your school with a sticker.
3. Each person should show where they live with named stickers.
4. Work out how far everyone travels to get to school. Estimate this by drawing a straight line directly from your house to school. Use the scale on the map to work out how far this is.
5. Do the people who live the furthest away take the longest time to get to school? If not, why not?
6. Compare the results for your class with others in your school.

Some schools are using their buildings and facilities to make extra money. Examples of ways to do this include renting out rooms for evening classes for adults. School children may help to raise money for their school with summer fairs and sponsored events. This helps schools survive in some areas.

A group of children at a small village school in Talconeston, Norfolk.

What services are there?

Villages have fewer **services** than towns. A service is a facility like a shop, a restaurant or garage; they enable us to carry on with our day-to-day lives. If there are no services like shops where you live, then you have to travel elsewhere to do your shopping. Villages only have a few services, as there aren't enough people to support the cost of running a large number of services over a period of time.

Local post offices provide an important service for many villages, but they are under threat.

Village shops were booming in the 1920s and 1930s, but once people started to own their own cars, it became easier for them to travel to towns with more shops and supermarkets that sold goods at lower prices. This meant that village shops lost customers, and struggled to make a **profit**. As a result, many village shops closed down.

How many services can you spot in the photograph shown?

In order to stay in business, village shop owners have had to think creatively. Some offer several services within the same shop. For example, a village shop could be a grocers, bakers and a post office all rolled into one.

With fewer village libraries, mobile libraries are an important service. Elderly people in villages who cannot drive especially benefit from mobile libraries and services such as meals-on-wheels, which brings food to their door. Local bus services help villagers who do not have cars to travel to their nearest town.

A mobile library provides a service for villagers who would otherwise have to travel to their nearest town to go to the library.

DETECTIVE WORK

Next time you pass through a village, count the number of services that you can see from the main road. In particular, look out for shops, churches and petrol stations. What types of services are available? Is it true that there are more services in larger villages? Can you explain this pattern?

What jobs do people do?

Within a village you find people doing a variety of different jobs to earn a living. Jobs include working in farming, tourism, or running a business from home. The mix of different jobs reflects how life in the countryside is changing: farming employs fewer people than in the past, so people need to find an alternative way of earning a living. Some people are employed within the village, while others have to leave each day to work elsewhere.

Farmers at a sheep auction in Ruthin, Clwyd.

Farming is important in **rural** areas. In recent years, farming has been under pressure, because of changes to the way farmers are paid. To boost their income, some farmers have converted old farm buildings into accommodation for tourists. Others open their farms for school visits, or have had wind farms built on their land. Using the Internet, farmers can sell produce directly to customers, avoiding shops and supermarkets.

FOCUS ON

A village potter

Elspeth Owen is a potter who lives and works in the village of Grantchester near Cambridge. Many of Grantchester's inhabitants work for Cambridge University, or commute to jobs beyond the village. Since 1975, Elspeth has worked in a former cricket pavilion that looks out over the meadows in Grantschester. In 2000, the pavilion was earmarked for conversion into a house by its owners. The pavilion was saved from development following a campaign led by Elspeth. To find out more, go to:

weblinks

www.waylinks.co.uk/series/
GeogDetective/Villages

**A train leaves Kings Sutton in Northamptonshire
taking people to their places of work outside the village.**

People may have to travel outside of the village in order to go and work in larger towns and cities. However, some people are choosing to locate their businesses in villages instead. One example is Oracle, an IT company based in Sonning in Berkshire. One of the reasons the company has chosen to locate in Sonning is that the village environment is felt to be cleaner and less busy than if it was located in a large town.

Why would a business want to locate to a village?

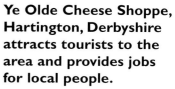

Ye Olde Cheese Shoppe, Hartington, Derbyshire attracts tourists to the area and provides jobs for local people.

What traditions do villagers celebrate?

Traditions, some of which have been performed for hundreds of years, are an important focus for many village communities.

Morris dancers in action in Grassington, Yorkshire.

Morris dancing is a tradition with a long history. Although there are several types of morris dancing, one of the best known is 'Cotswold Morris'. It developed in the villages of the Cotswold Hills around Oxfordshire and Gloucestershire. Teams are made up of six male dancers, a musician and a person dressed as an animal. Each village develops its own special dance steps, which are named after their village. Performances include handkerchief, clapping and stick dances performed by men in white clothes and bells worn below the knee.

DETECTIVE WORK
Find out about village traditions in an area near to where you live. What are people celebrating and how are they celebrating?

Dancers weave ribbons around a maypole on the village green in Ickwell Green, Bedfordshire.

While there are many important events in village life, two stand out: May Day and **Guy Fawkes** night. May Day originally marked the day when cattle were sent into the fields after spending the winter in barns. In villages such as Ickwell Green in Bedfordshire, couples dance around a **maypole** weaving ribbons around a coloured post to mark the beginning of celebrations and dancing.

As in many other **settlements**, villagers celebrate Guy Fawkes night (5th November). The evening is often managed by a village committee who arrange for a giant bonfire to be built on the **village green**, together with a 'Guy' and fireworks.

FOCUS ON

Grasmere

Grasmere, in Cumbria, sees a variety of traditions take place in summer. In August, people gather to watch a rush-bearing ceremony performed by village children. This ceremony originates from the days when the local church had an earth floor that was covered in rushes. Grasmere sports are celebrated in the summer, with competitions in **fell running**.

Competitors tumble downhill in pursuit of a rolling Double Gloucester Cheese, as local people spectate.

What might the people in the bottom photograph be celebrating?

What plants and animals live in villages?

Villages and their surrounding areas are rich in different wildlife. **Habitats** include river banks that are home to animals such as water voles, kingfishers, dragonflies and plants like wild garlic and water mint. Other village habitats to look out for include overgrown fields, wild meadows, ponds and marshes.

Churchyards are full of plants and animals. They often contain voles, shrews and wild flowers, like celandine. They have a range of different lichens and mosses which grow well on tombstones. Ancient woodlands such as Hayley Wood, near Longstowe, Cambridgeshire, are home to different species of fungi, insects, birds, and flowers, like bluebells and dog's mercury.

Why is this churchyard a good habitat for wildlife?

The churchyard in Tilford village, Surrey, has been allowed to grow wild, though the paths remain clear.

Rabbits often make their homes in woodland areas.

Many villages are famous for their gardens. Originally created to grow herbs used for medicine and cooking, gardens were also used to grow vegetables and flowers. Village gardens are entered into a range of garden competitions across the country. Winners proudly announce their success on village signs.

Villages in **rural** areas are often good places to find hedgerows. Hedgerows provide an excellent habitat for many animals, from nesting birds to mice. In some areas where hedgerows have been cut down to make way for building developments, efforts have been made to restore hedgerows in order to bring back important habitats.

A hedgerow lines a country lane along the edge of a woodland in Surrey.

How do villages change?

One major trend that is changing villages is that of people moving to **rural** villages from larger towns and cities. People are attracted to countryside villages as they believe that they offer a better quality of life: cleaner air, less crime and beautiful scenery.

A house advertised for sale near Lechlade in the Cotswolds.

Relatively wealthy families from **urban** areas are moving into rural areas, putting a demand on the housing supply. In turn, this pushes up the average cost of a house in the village. Some people are concerned that this pressure for housing will lead to more homes being built, which could change the character and sense of community within many villages.

This situation has led to the development of **dormitory villages** where residents leave the village to go and work elsewhere during the day, but return to sleep in the village during the evening. This can make villages seem deserted during daylight hours.

For some families living and working in rural villages, a lack of money can be a problem. One in five rural households has a below average income. This is partly because of the decline in money made by farming. The decline in the range of **services** provided by villages also presents a problem. In 1999, 75% of rural villages did not have a bus service, 42% didn't have a shop, 43% were without a post office and 49% had no school.

However, many new people who move into a village bring valuable skills to their community, such as expertise in running businesses which could help villages in the long term. New village residents are also encouraged to support the activities that define village life by joining local clubs and supporting local schools and shops. Efforts are being made in some villages to build new houses that fit in well with the older buildings in the area.

Village residents support a summer fête in the village of Longworth, Oxfordshire.

What is Wharram Percy?

Villages have experienced changes throughout the past. For example, there are thousands of villages in Great Britain that are now deserted, such as Wharram Percy. Many of these deserted villages originated during **medieval** times. The changes that led to their desertion include changes to farming and how people make money – similar reasons for the changes experienced by villages today.

Wharram Percy, located in Yorkshire, is Europe's most famous deserted medieval village. The Yorkshire village dates back to the Iron Age, but was abandoned around 1500 AD.

A picture of how Wharram Percy might have looked in the 1400s.

During medieval times, Wharram Percy was home to people who made a living by farming the land to grow crops for food. Houses were different to the type of houses that you find in most villages today – they had just one storey and sometimes housed cattle as well as people. Religion was very important to people during medieval times, and so the church was an important focus for the community, especially on Sundays – as it still is in many villages.

Wharram Percy today: the remains of the church.

Today, all that remains of the village is a ruined church, grassy lanes and building foundations overgrown with plants. The village was deserted as a result of changes to farming. Wharram Percy was originally a centre for crop farming. However, the growing of crops was gradually replaced with sheep farming in the village as it made more money. Sheep wool was needed to supply the growing wool industry across the country. The houses that people lived in were knocked down to make way for fields used to graze sheep.

DETECTIVE WORK

Investigate how a village near to where you live has changed in the last few years. You could research the following ideas:

1. How has the range of **services** changed? For example, are there new shops or have some had to close?
2. How regular is the local bus service? How has it changed?
3. Where do adults in your local village work? How is this different to 50 years ago?

What is the future for villages?

Changes to villages are being driven by the developments in farming. Fewer people are needed to farm the land leading to the loss of jobs, the use of machines has seen fields expand and chemicals that control pests and weeds have damaged our natural wildlife. Villages are under pressure to extend the supply of housing because of a growing **population** and a lack of existing housing.

Tourism is important for the future of villages, providing jobs and a new source of income. Villagers have set up small businesses, such as bed and breakfasts and gift shops, to cater for tourists who need a wide range of **services**. However, some people argue that tourism brings pollution, crime and high house prices.

Community volunteers work together to clean up their village surroundings.

The CPRE (the Campaign to Protect Rural England) is one organisation that has worked to protect many **rural** villages since 1926. The CPRE has campaigned to minimise the spread of built-up areas, to promote the green belt (areas of countryside around large **urban** areas that are protected from large scale building) and the creation of **national parks**. Some local councils are involved in a series of initiatives to help preserve important areas of interest in villages. For example, West Dorset District Council is creating conservation areas – places of historic interest that are protected so that people can enjoy them in the future. The council is working with local people to ensure that their views are represented when decisions about this are made.

Many people care about the future of villages and are actively working to sustain old traditions and develop new ones. For example, lots of villages were involved in campaigns to commemorate the Millennium through the planting of trees, and the building of village halls and playgrounds.

Wanborough Church, Surrey undergoes conservation work on its tower.

Your project

You will now know lots of things about villages in Britain. Why not investigate different villages around the world? You could research the types of houses that people live in; look at different traditions that have survived; or investigate how villages are coping with changes in the world around them.

Sherlock Bones travelled to several villages in Romania. In the region of Maramures he found villages where families had lived for generations. Homes are made of oak or pine, roofs are tall and steep, and some, like in England, are thatched. Some houses have huge gates with detailed pictures carved into them. Villagers celebrate a folk music festival called 'Hora de la Prislop', held on the second Sunday in August, where people dance, sing and play music on traditional instruments.

A village scene in Marmures, Romania.

Project presentation

- You could build a model using modelling clay of the village you have studied to show what it is like.

- See whether you can find maps and satellite images of your chosen village using Google Earth.
  For more information, go to:

  weblinks

  www.waylinks.co.uk/series/
  GeogDetective/Villages

- Recreate some of the activities (such as dances) that people do in villages around the world with your class at school.

- Create a photo journal to explain a day in the life of a person in your chosen village.

Cattle are herded in and out of a Masai village in Kenya.

Glossary

Almshouse Houses that are built and managed by charities to house those who are poor.

Cul-de-sac A housing estate, often with one end blocked off.

Dispersed A type of settlement pattern where buildings are spread far apart.

Dormitory village A name given to a type of village where the majority of inhabitants leave the village to go and work elsewhere during the day, returning in the evening.

Fell-running A form of 'extreme' cross country running across mountainous areas.

Flooding A flood occurs when the water in a river channel flows over its banks.

Guy Fawkes A man who unsuccessfully tried to blow up parliament in 1605.

Habitats An area that supports a particular type of plant or animal.

Limestone A grey/white sedimentary rock made from calcium carbonate.

Linear A name given to a type of village that has developed in a long, thin shape along a river, road or valley.

Maypole A tall pole with ribbons attached at one end. Dancers weave a canopy of ribbons around the pole.

Medieval The historical period from the years 1066-1500.

National park An area of land in the countryside that is protected from development and building work because of its beauty or wildlife.

Nucleated A type of settlement pattern where buildings are clustered around a central place like a road junction.

Population The people who live in a particular place.

Profit The amount of money that a business has made once its bills have been paid.

Rural An area of countryside.

Services The shops, facilities and leisure activities that help people in their everyday lives. Examples include shops, post offices, dry cleaners and shoe menders.

Settlement A place where people have constructed buildings to live in.

Site The place where a settlement is built.

Terrace A type of housing where rows of houses are built and the houses are attached to each other on both sides.

Thatching A traditional method used to build roofs out of natural materials such as reeds or heather.

Urban An area that is very built up such as a town or a city.

Village green An area of grassland, sometimes with a pond that is usually in the centre of a village. In the past, greens were sometimes used by people to graze animals but today, they are normally just used for recreation.

Answers

Page 7 On page 6 the village shown is linear and on page 7 the village shown is nucleated.

Page 14 A grocery shop, post office and lottery sales are three different services offered within the same building.

Page 17 A clean environment, green surroundings, peaceful area, less congestion from traffic and lower land prices.

Page 19 They are celebrating the making of new cheeses in Gloucestershire by taking part in the local tradition of cheese rolling.

Page 20 The churchyard has been left alone for a long time, so wildlife has not been disturbed. Unlike many areas of open countryside, churchyards are less likely to me contaminated with chemicals like pesticides and fertilisers from farming.

Further Information

Books to read

Rural Britain: Then & Now
by Roger Hunt
(Cassell, 2006)

The English Village
by Leigh Driver
(New Holland Publishers, 2005)

Exploring Villages
by Katie Orchard
(Wayland, 2004)

Lonely Planet guides for research about villages abroad.

Websites:

For more information about the village of Wharram Percy:
http://www.uk360s.co.uk/360-viewer/index.php?gallery=north-yorkshire/wharram_percy

For more information about CPRE:
http://www.cpre.org.uk/

General wildlife sites:
http://www.wildlifetrusts.org/
http://www.wildlifebritain.com/

Index

The Geography Detective Investigates

Contents of all books in the series:

WAYLAND